COLOR YOURSEL

Calmness

& reduce stress with your animal spirits

Adult Coloring Book

Original artwork by **Sue Coccia**

CICO BOOKS

LONDON NEW YORK

Published in 2023 by CICO Books
An imprint of Ryland Peters & Small Ltd
20–21 Jockey's Fields   341 E 116th St
London WC1R 4BW   New York, NY 10029

www.rylandpeters.com

10 9 8 7 6 5 4 3 2 1

First published in 2015

ISBN: 978-1-80065-270-5

Printed in China

Senior editor: Carmel Edmonds
Art director: Sally Powell
Creative director: Leslie Harrington
Head of production: Patricia Harrington
Publishing manager: Penny Craig
Publisher: Cindy Richards

Contents

Introduction

Award-winning Northwest artist Sue Coccia lives in Edmonds, Washington, in a picturesque setting to be envied, where orcas practically swim up to her doorstep, the smell of saltwater gives off a memorable scent, and you can set your watch to the gentle tuba-like sounds announcing ferry boat arrivals. It is here that Sue gets her inspiration to draw the natural wonders that share the surrounding mountains and waterways. With her trademark Pacific Northwest Totem Art, Sue shepherds animals onto paper or a canvas much like Noah ushered them onto his ark. Her depictions of ladybugs, frogs, bears, raccoons, and everything else indigenous to each region march two by two, with all sorts of clever storylines playing out inside the crisp outlines of her favorite creatures. The animals are integrated into these different settings as if willingly moving through a challenging maze. The rest of us get to sit back and look at their souls.

Take, for example, Frog (see page 48). Frog represents prosperity, healing, and inner peace. In the center is the great inner strength of Bear, who is living abundantly along with the love and protection of Turtle. Dragonfly enters Frog's dreams to bring about transformation and enlightenment. Journey within Frog as you express your individuality like Whale, and gain the power of Snake. Good luck and happiness are yours with Ladybug!

Each illustration is drawn by hand in pen and ink: Sue chooses which animal to draw, but does not draw the outline, and plans it only in her mind. Instead, she starts in the middle and works outward, incorporating intricate imagery and developing the story. Finally, she adds the outline, creating a spectacular and meaningful artwork.

Sue has been a professional artist for more than two decades and received her formal training at Seattle's respected Burnley School for Professional Art. She compares drawing to meditating, and the results are as calming and soothing to her as they are to those who seek them out. Her love of animals at an early age encouraged her to nurture and protect them while giving her an artistic theme. She holds memberships in countless wildlife organizations, among them the Orca Network, Bats Northwest, International Crane Foundation, and International Wolf Center.

It takes an interesting woman to view the world differently than the rest of us, and Sue is all of that. She understands true love, meeting her husband Frank on the first day of high school and enjoying a relationship going on four-plus decades now, and that deep passion comes across in her art. Diversity is another unmistakable element in her drawings, and that is an offshoot of her Native American background; her grandmother was Cherokee, giving Sue a full appreciation for different cultures and mores. She uses Native American, Polynesian, and Aboriginal images to show that we're all connected in some manner.

She is a highly disciplined person in so many ways, holding a black belt in Tae Kwon Do. She is a devoted gardener, an activity that gave her a strong affinity for ladybugs and her signature stroke: She incorporates the lovable insect into each one of her drawings.

No one sees and duplicates the world quite like Sue.

Desert

COYOTE playfulness, trickster, humor

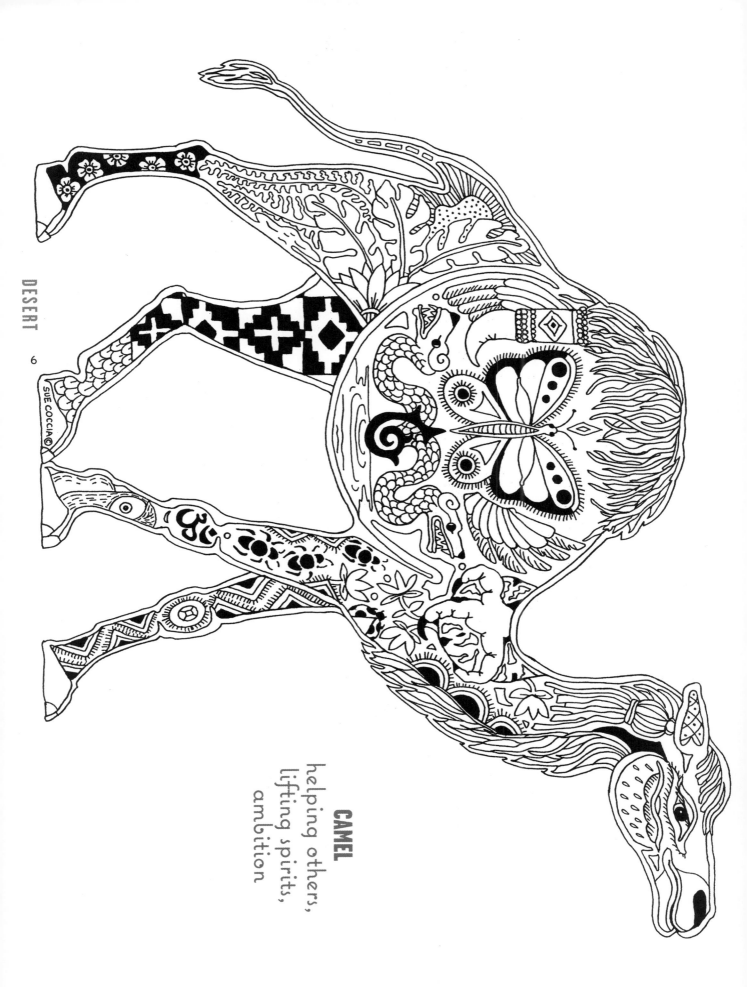

SUE COCCIA©

CAMEL
helping others,
lifting spirits,
ambition

PHOENIX rejuvenation, peace, prosperity

ROADRUNNER
courage, quick
thinking, swiftness

· SUE COCCIA ®··

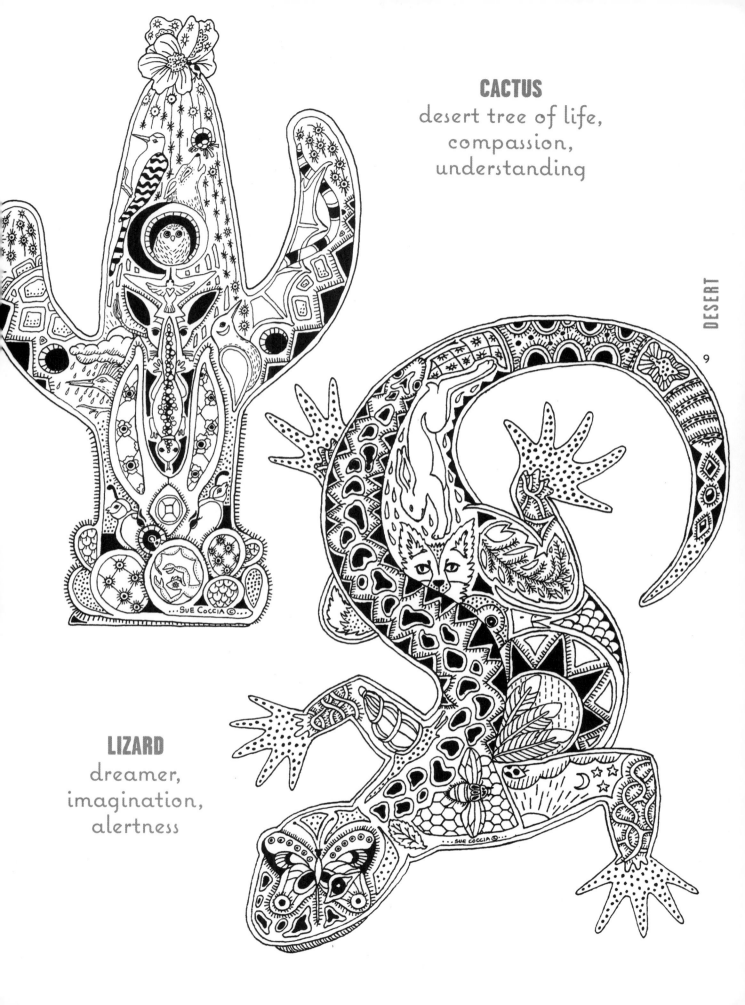

CACTUS
desert tree of life,
compassion,
understanding

LIZARD
dreamer,
imagination,
alertness

SCARAB clairvoyance, resurrection, good luck

SUE COCCIA © 2001

SNAKE *creativity, change, confidence*

THUNDERBIRD *power, intelligence, compassion*

DESERT TORTOISE protection, longevity, wisdom

Prairie and Savannah

SUE COCCIA . . ©

DORMOUSE success, alertness, scrutiny

DEER gentleness, love, caring

SUE COCCIA

BEE productivity, harmony, bliss

HARE watchfulness, nurture, releasing fears

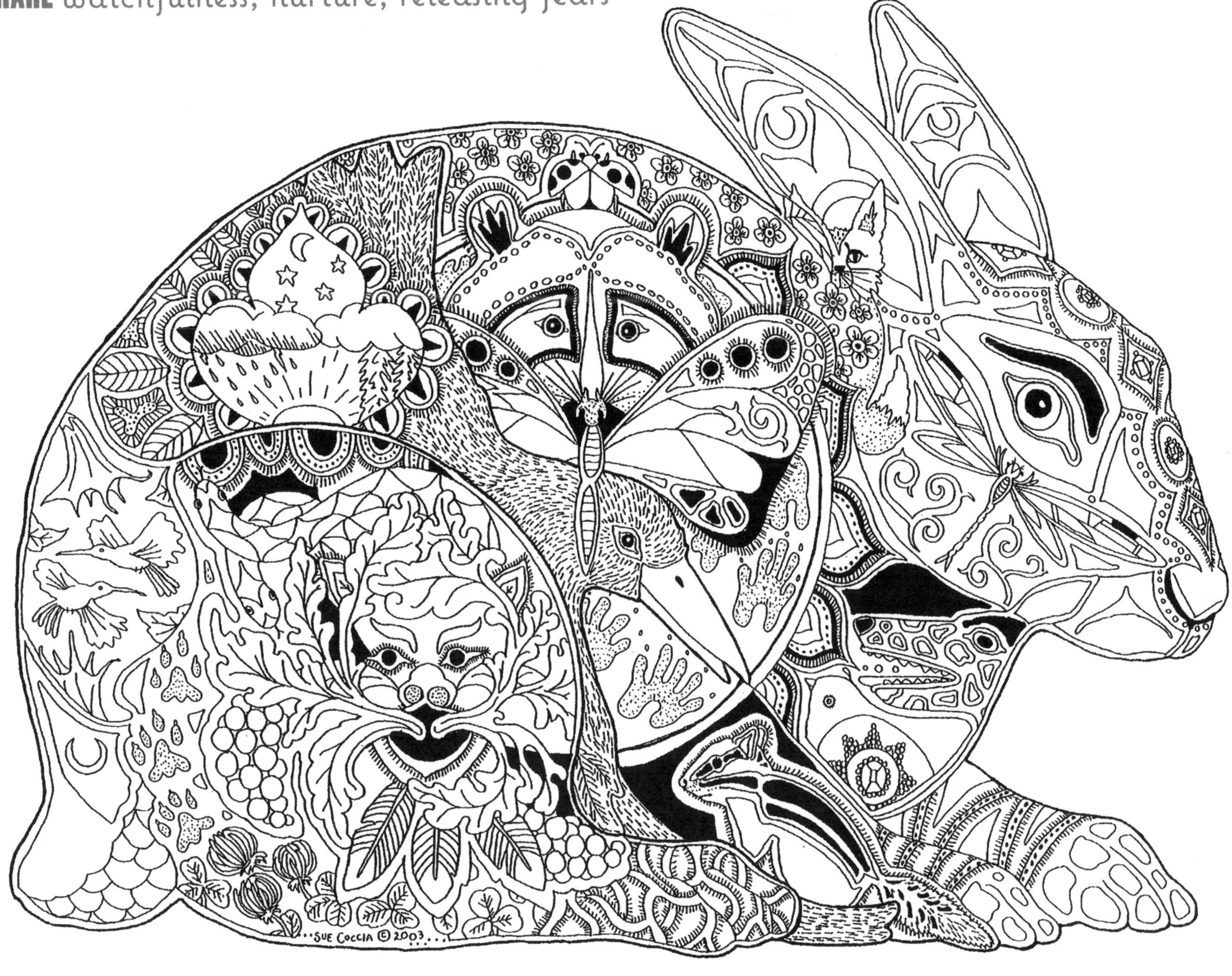

HAWK messenger, warrior, healing

HORSE power, freedom, balance

BUFFALO
gratitude,
power,
abundance

SUE COCCIA

SUE COCCIA

RAVEN magic, creativity, courage

ROOSTER drama, good reputation, watchfulness

QUAIL groundedness, courage, abundance

JAVELINA
opportunism,
expression,
intelligence

Mountains and Woodland

FOX cleverness, cunning, adaptation

BIG HORN SHEEP energy, determination, balance

BAT rebirth,
good luck,
sensitivity

LUNA MOTH sensitivity,
dreaming, intuition

CHIPMUNK *playfulness, confidence, survival*

WOODPECKER *protection, communication, fertility*

ELK stamina,
strength,
gentleness

SUE COCCIA

ARCTIC FOX observation, stealthiness, survival

EAGLE illumination, divine connection, courage

COUGAR leader, power, responsibility

MOUNTAINS AND WOODLAND

35

© SUE COCCIA

LOVEBIRDS transformation, Yin and Yang, peace

MOOSE
strength, self-esteem, maturity

OWL wisdom, vision, truth

GRIZZLY BEAR *meditation, healing, power*

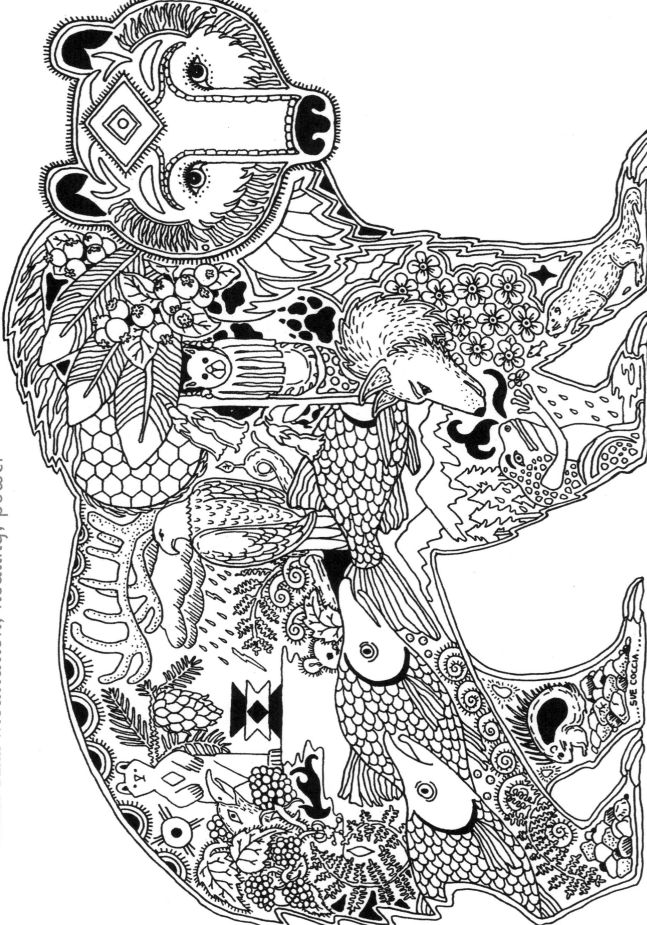

SUE COCCIA

RAVEN transformation, rebirth, playfulness

LYNX *secrecy, alertness, sensitivity*

RACCOON opportunism, curiosity, sociability

MUSK OX endurance, determination, service

Sue Coccia

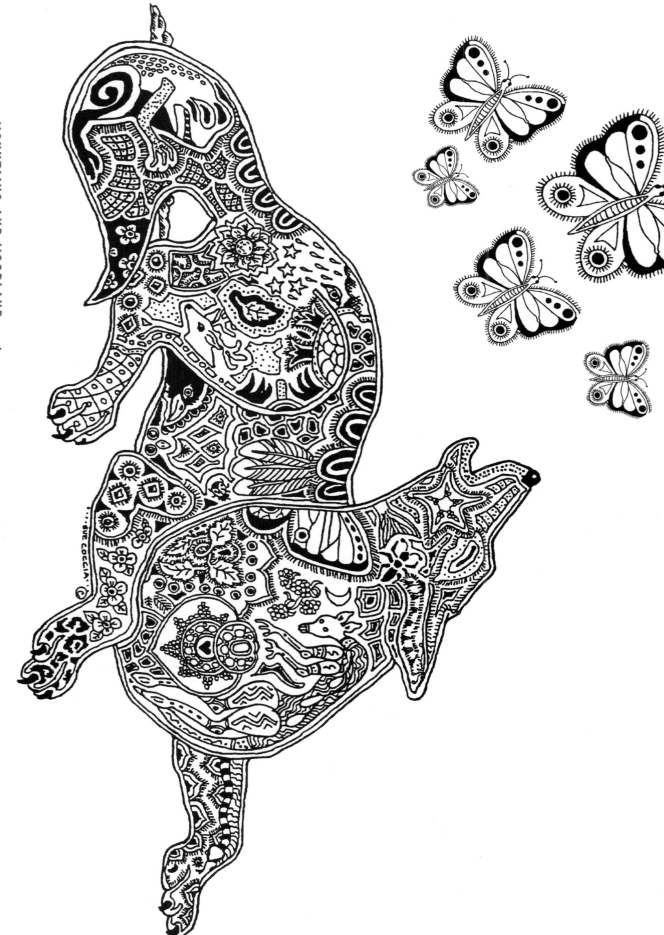

RAVEN AND BEAR
friendship,
strength,
watchfulness

REINDEER *endurance, abundance, determination*

WOLF path finder, spirit, balance

47

Sue Coccia

Rainforest

FROG prosperity, healing, inner peace

BUTTERFLIES transformation, beauty, joy

HUMMINGBIRD
joy, magic,
beauty

ROSE transformation,
beauty, delicacy

JAGUAR strength, healer, patience

GORILLA protector, peace, sociability

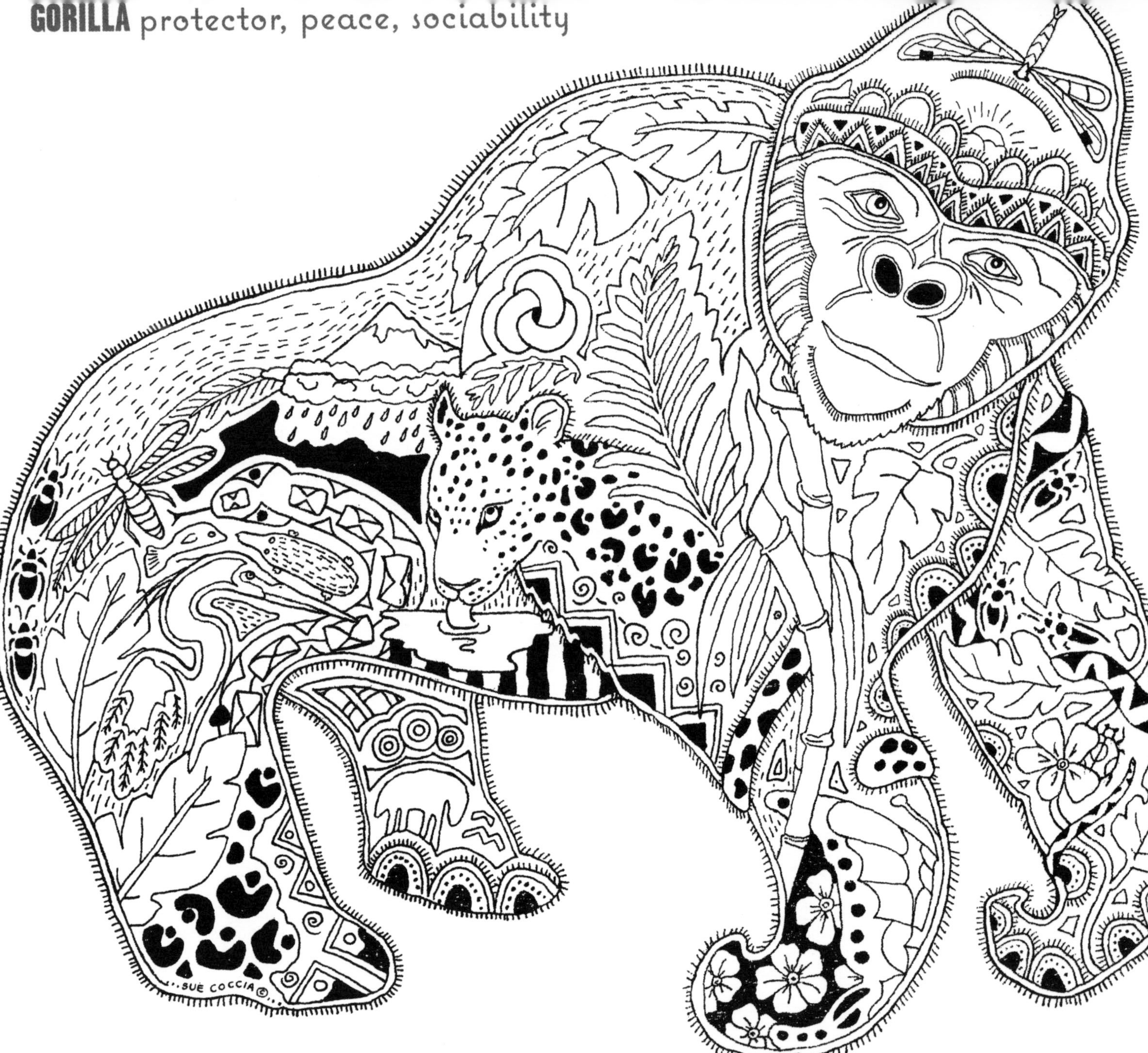

MACAW creativity, perception, sociability

LADYBUG good luck, happiness, joy

PEACOCK beauty, self-assurance, renewal

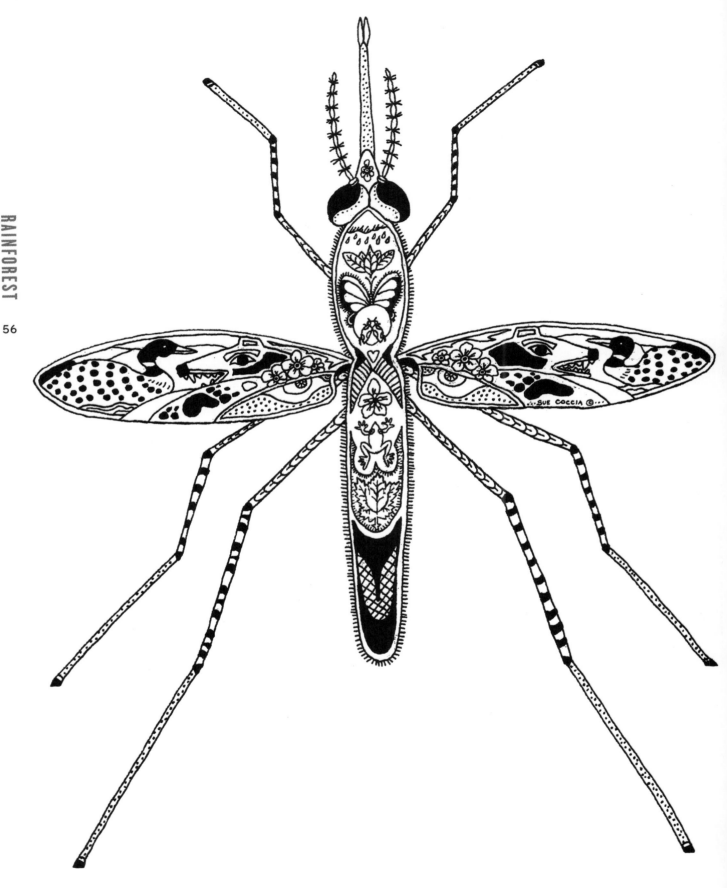

MOSQUITO agility, persistence, assertiveness

HUMMINGBIRD happiness, joy, beauty

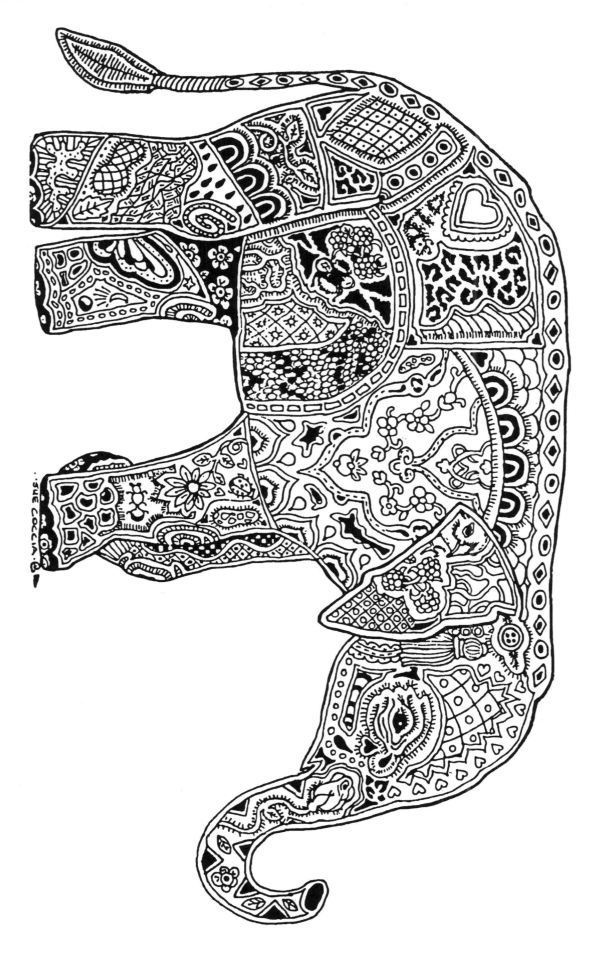

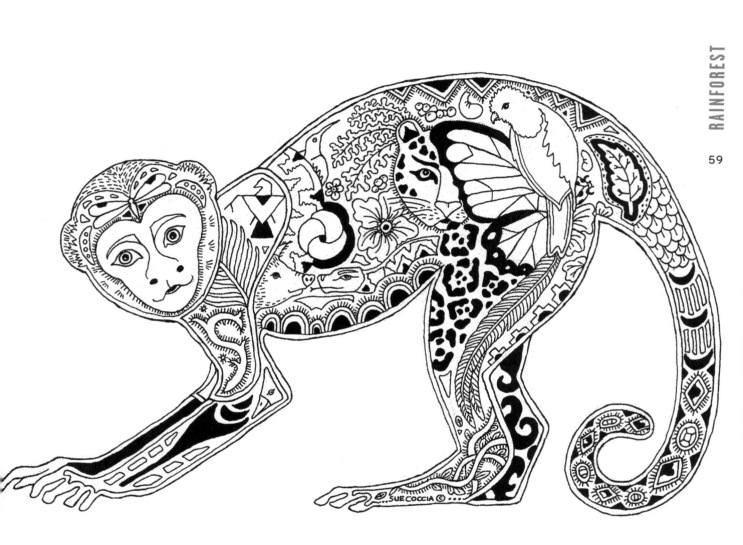

MONKEY playfulness, community, good health

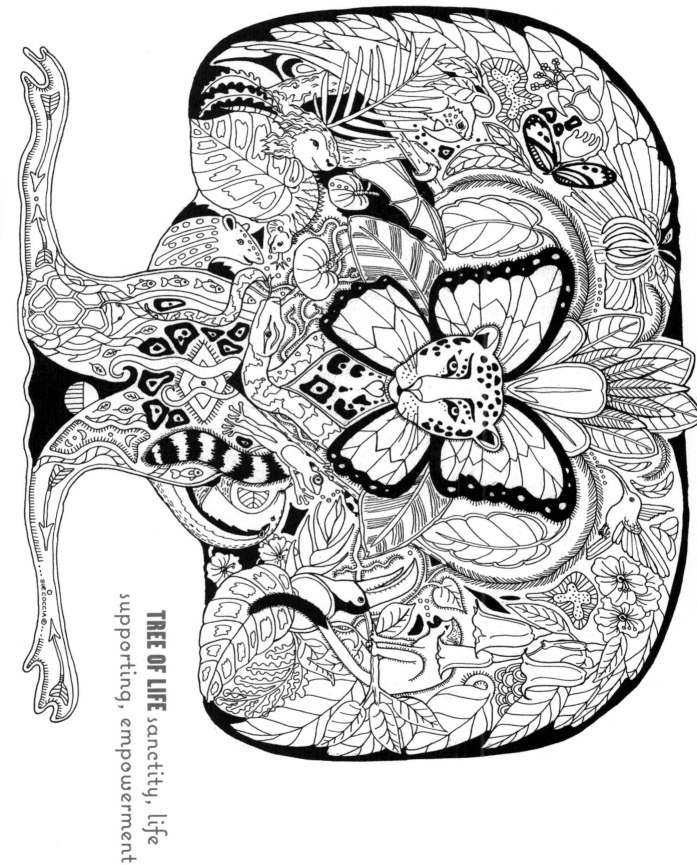

TREE OF LIFE sanctity, life
supporting, empowerment

TOUCAN expression, confidence, incarnation

TARANTULA *creativity, protection, change*

Rivers and Wetlands

CRANE longevity, focus, protection

DRAGONFLY *enlightenment, wisdom, transformation*

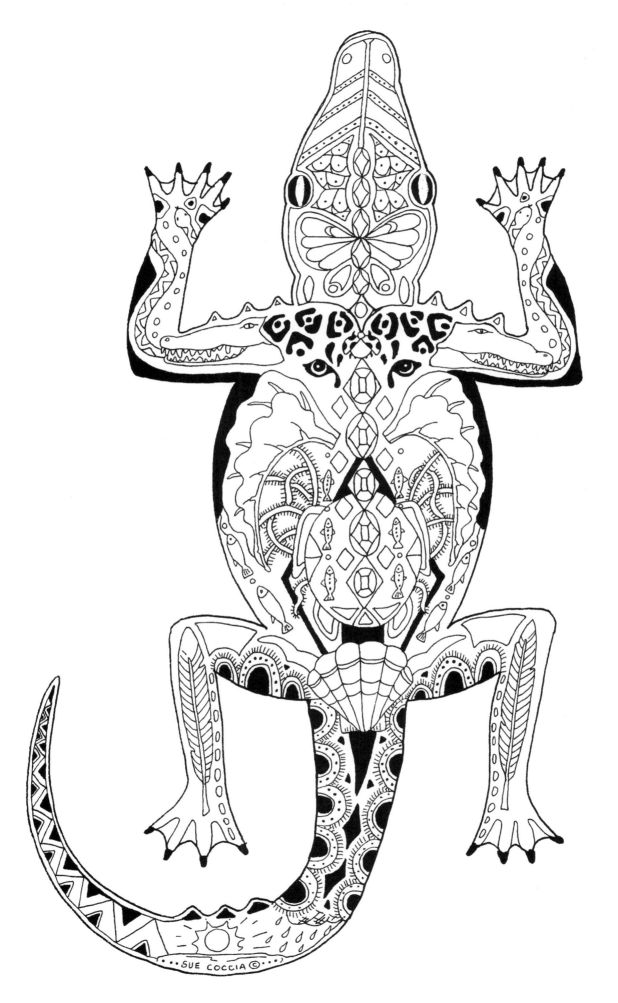

CROCODILE instinct, protection, strength

SUE COCCIA ©

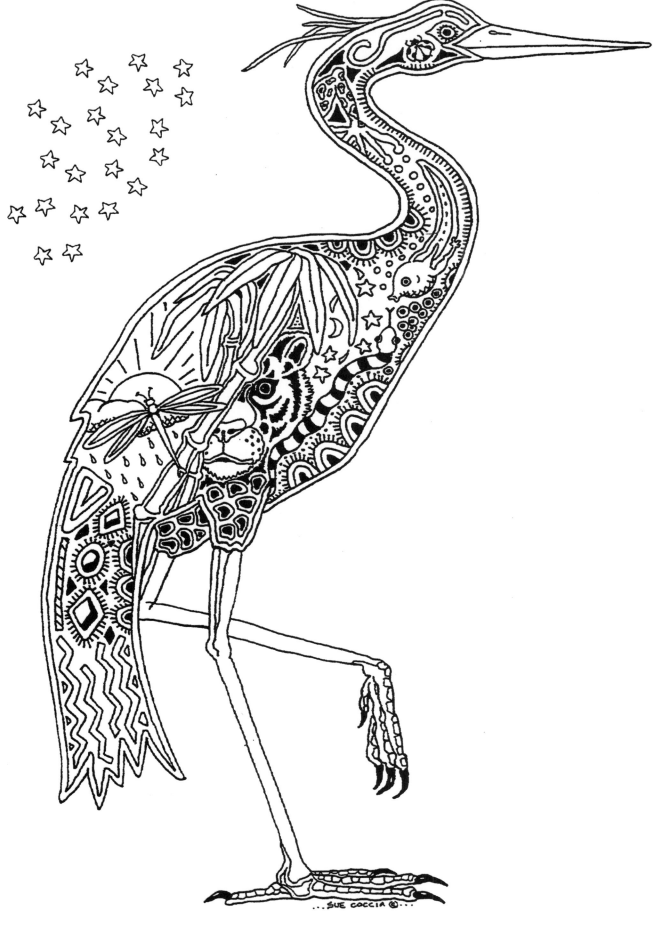

HERON balance, stability, determination

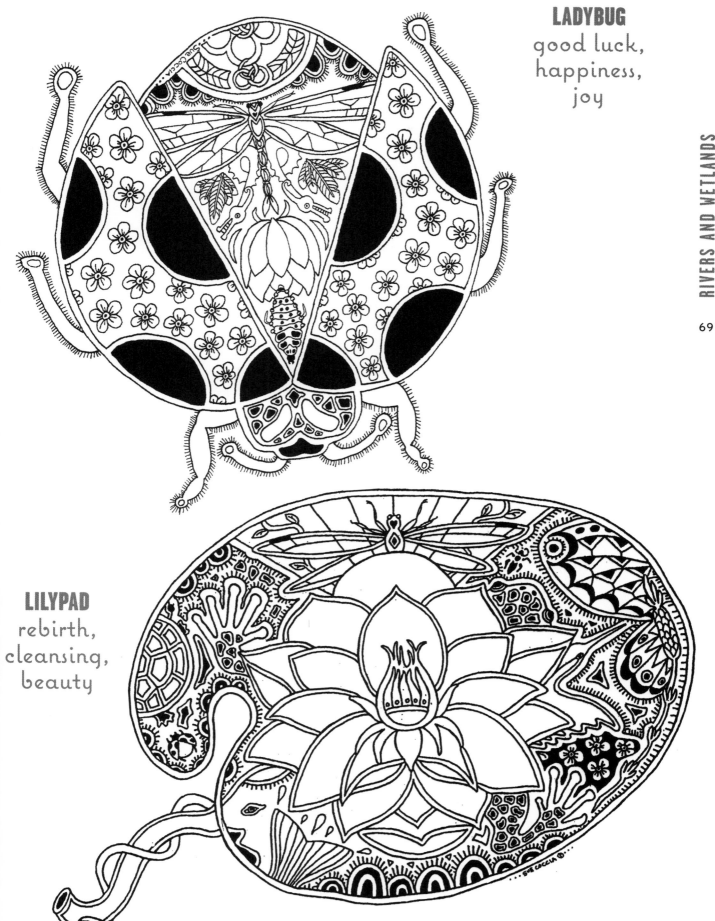

LADYBUG
good luck,
happiness,
joy

LILYPAD
rebirth,
cleansing,
beauty

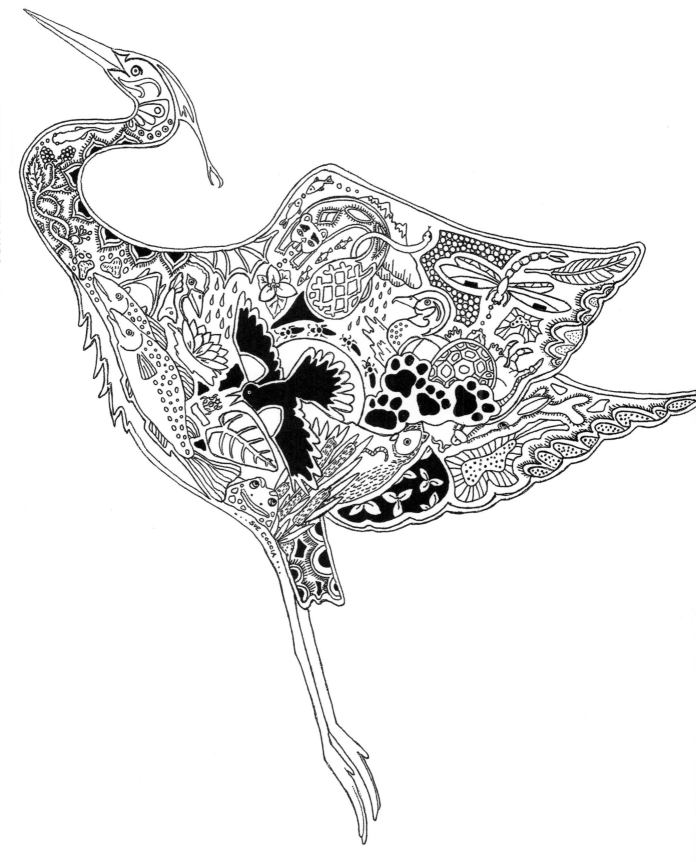

GREAT BLUE HERON groundedness, boundaries, sanctity

SWAN grace, love, awakening

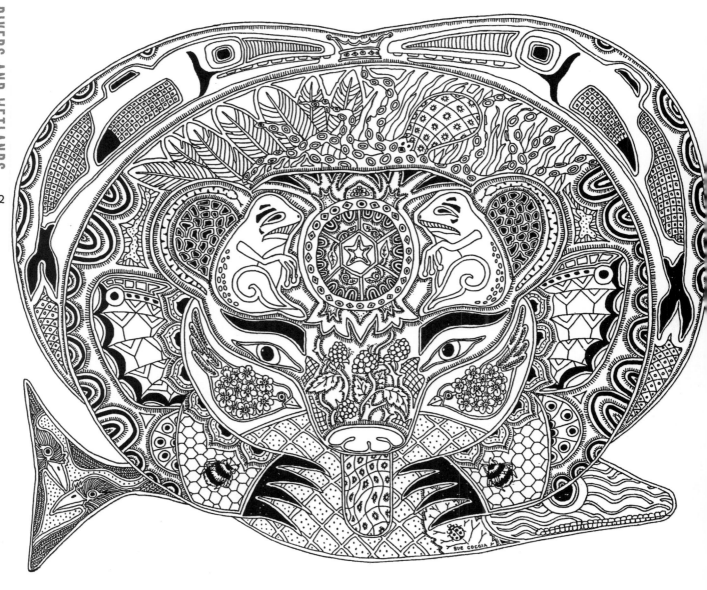

BIG RUMP BEAR (YAKWAWIAK) *power, strength, groundedness*

OTTER playfulness, joy, curiosity

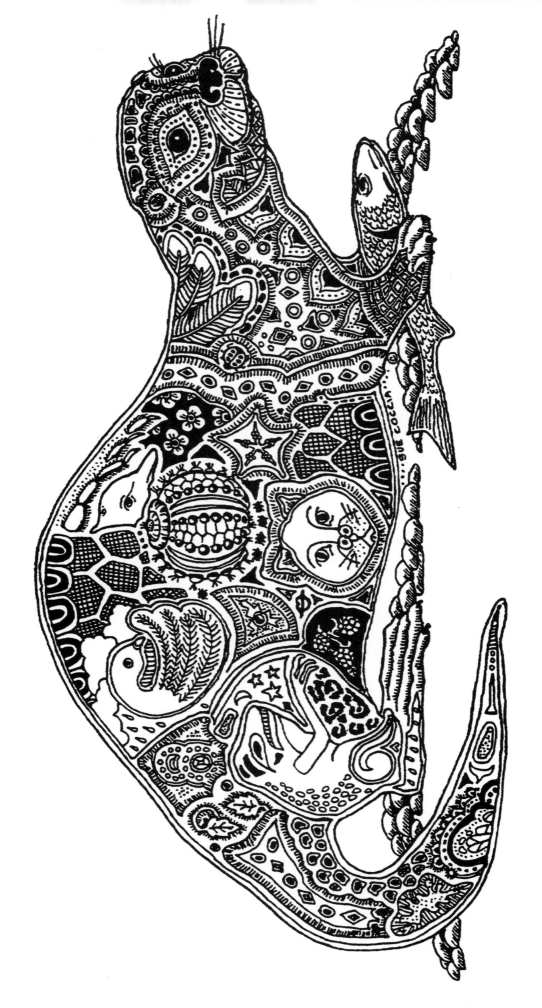

Oceans and Seas

BLUE WHALE great wisdom, intuition, breath

DOLPHIN joy, playfulness, harmony

CRAB tenacity, invention, creativity

CHINOOK AND SALMON transformation, determination, survival

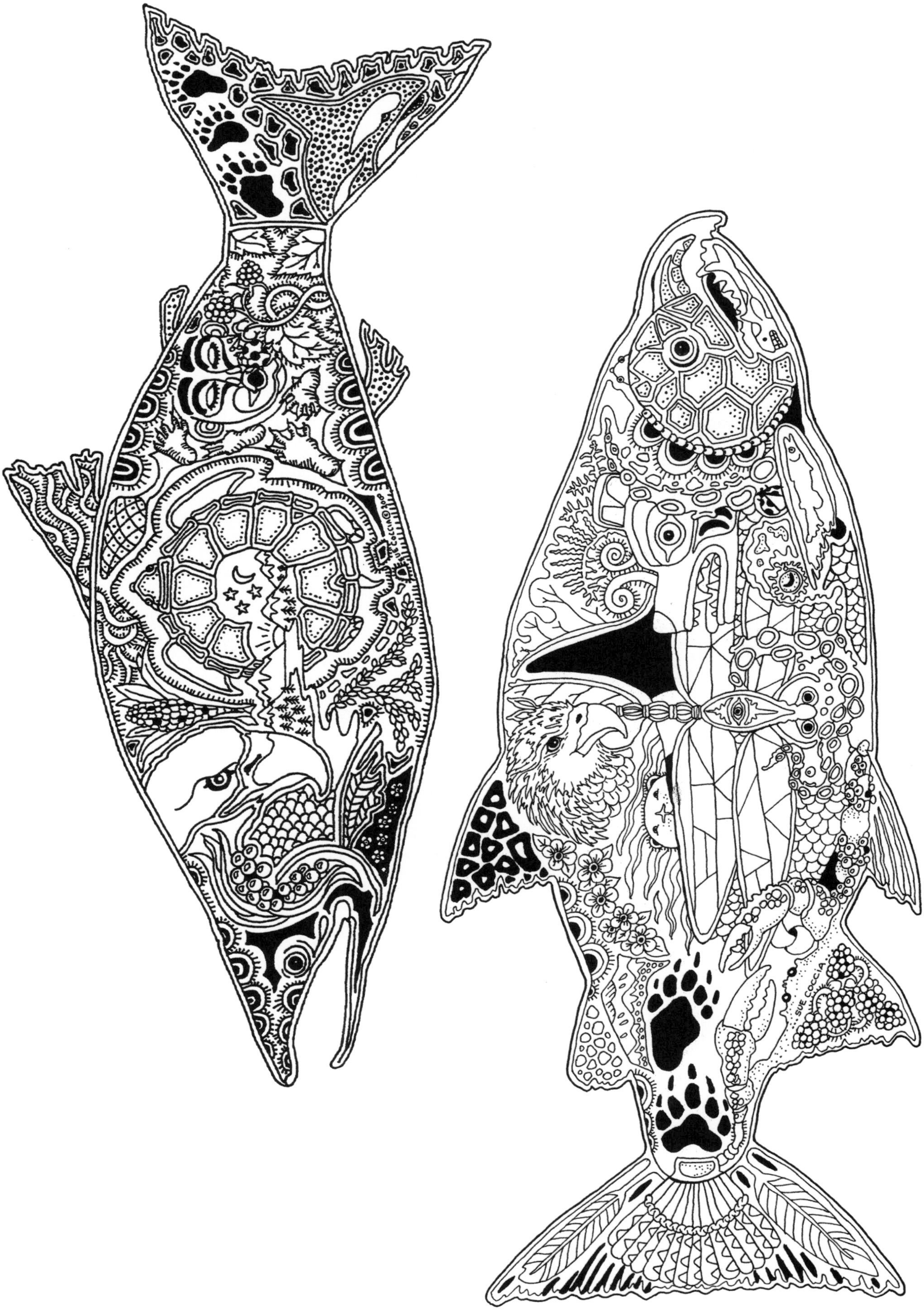

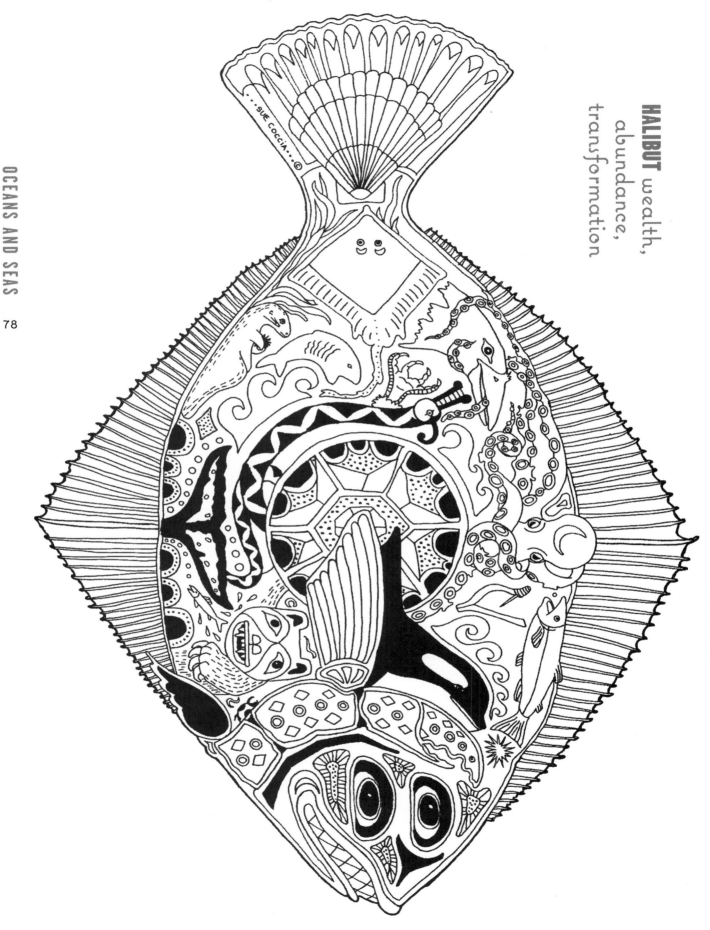

HALIBUT wealth, abundance, transformation

DALL'S PORPOISE community, harmony, gentleness

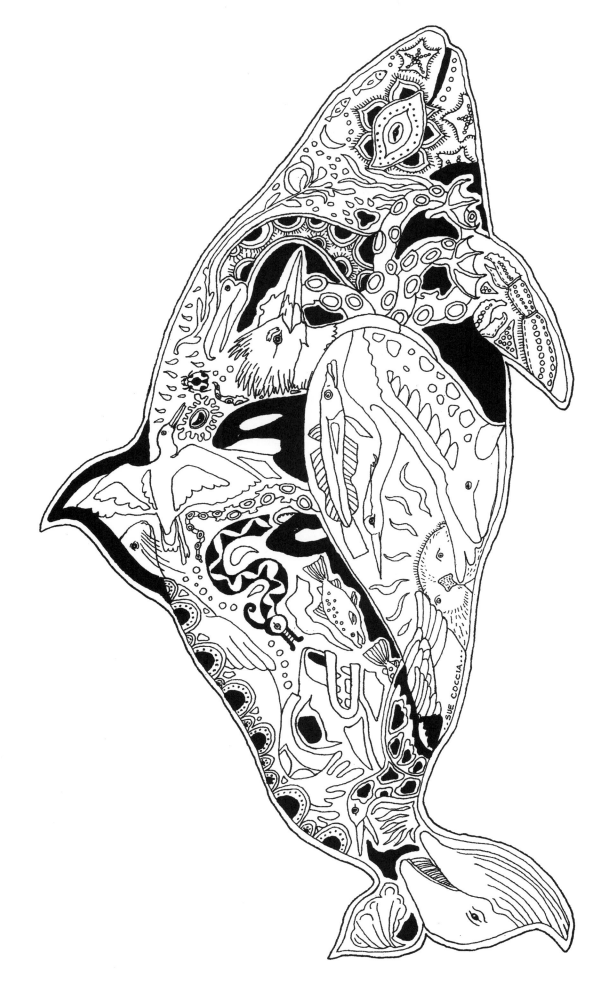

SUE COCCIA

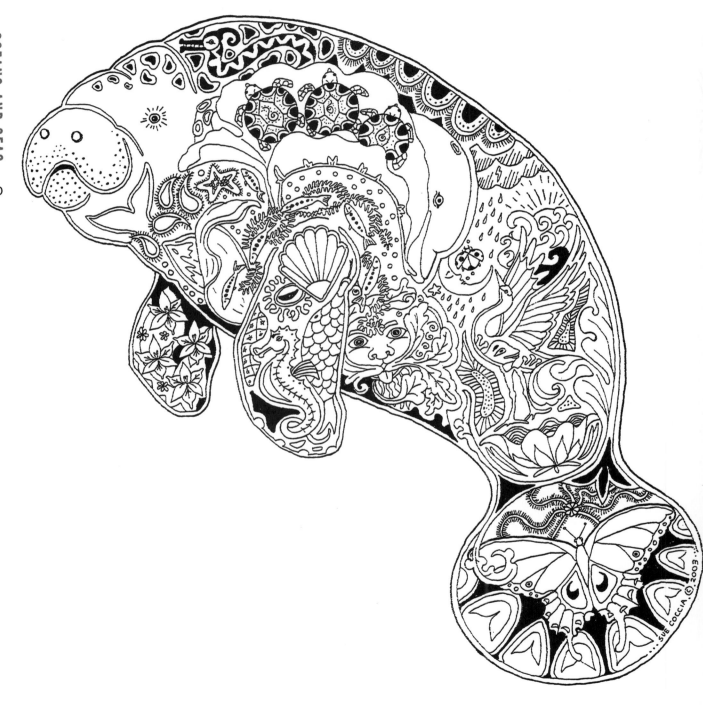

MANATEE trust, gentleness, guardian

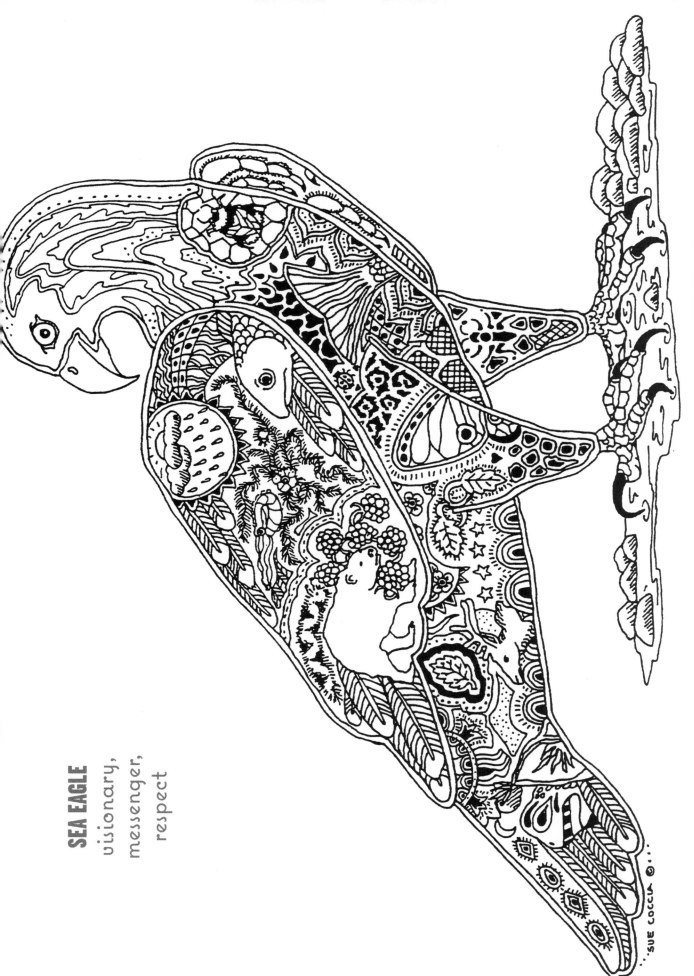

SEA EAGLE
visionary, messenger, respect

SUE COCCIA ©

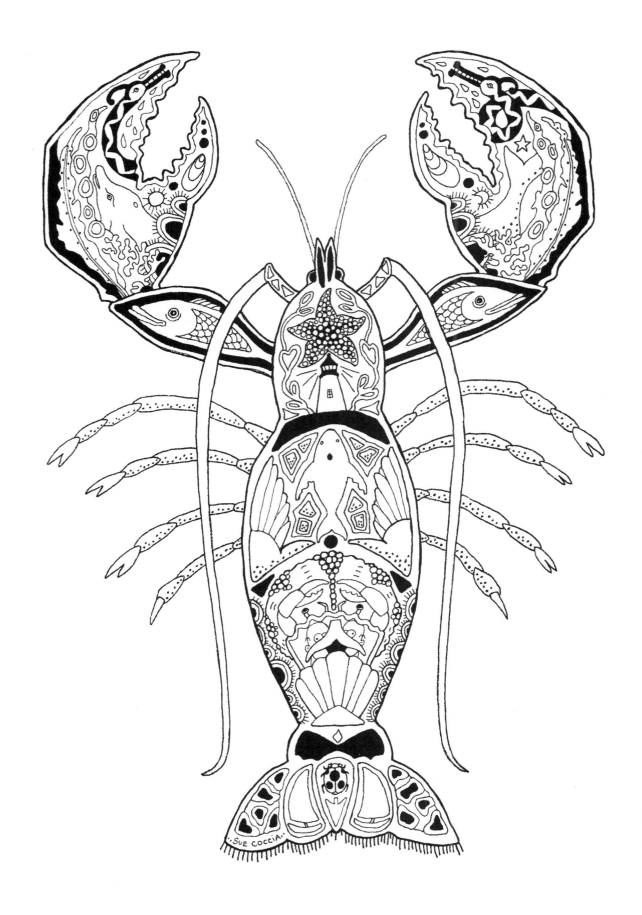

LOBSTER *vulnerability, regeneration, abundance*

OCTOPUS shyness, creativity, intelligence

ORCA
family,
power,
longevity

SHARK survivor,
protector, mystery

... SUE COCCIA ... ©

... SUE COCCIA ...

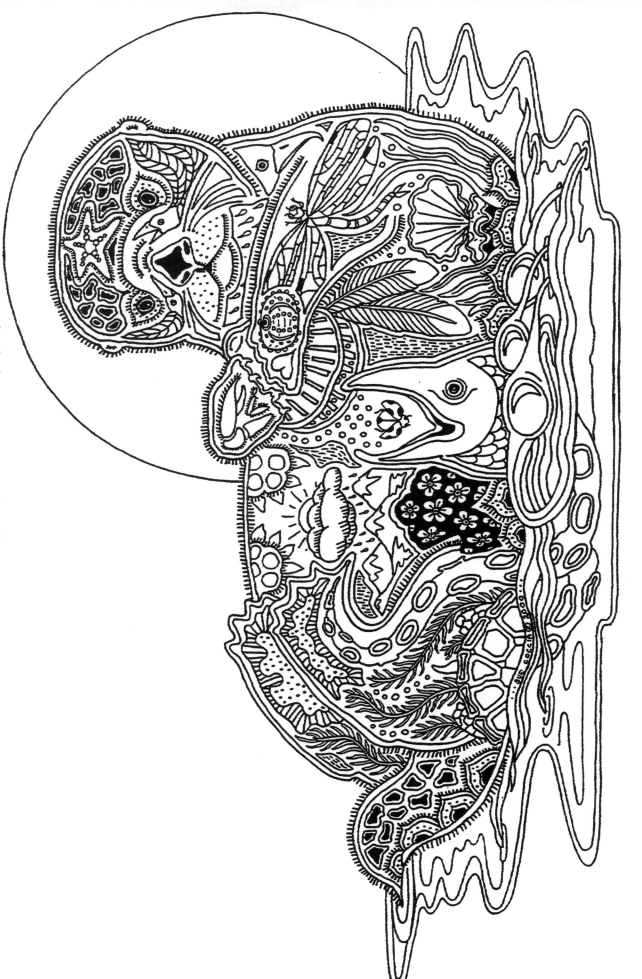

86

PUFFIN long life, companionship, relationships

SUE COCCIA ©2002

SEAHORSE protection, patience, awareness

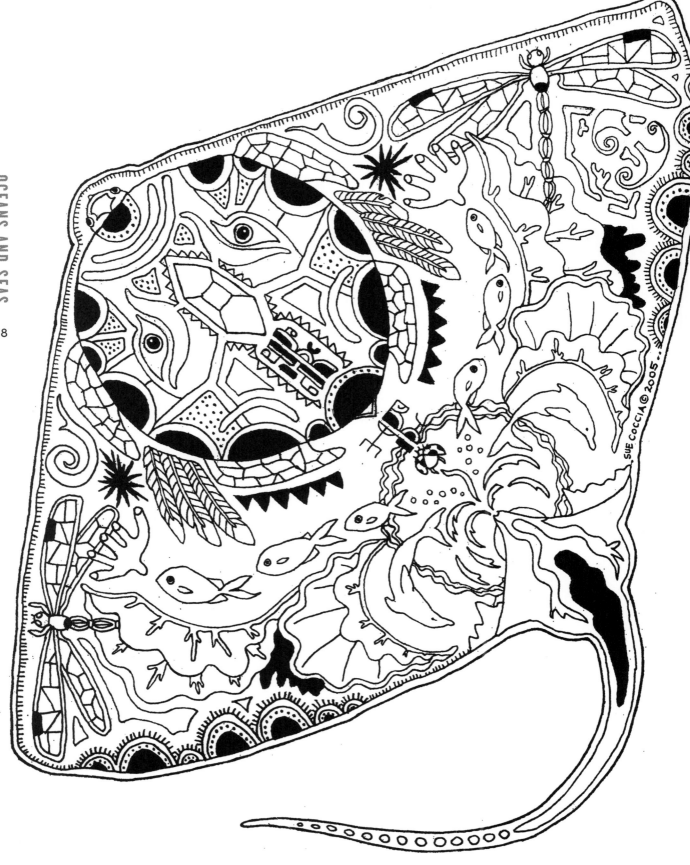

STINGRAY balance, grace, tenacity

PENGUIN *sociability, self-confidence, good etiquette*

WHELK
comfort,
trust,
shyness

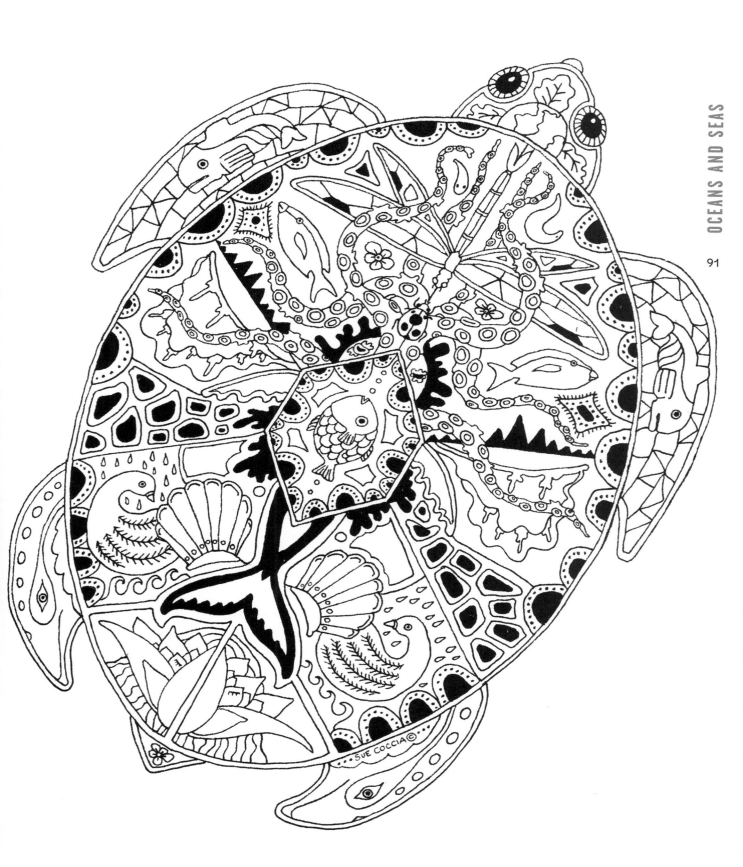

SEA TURTLE wisdom, longevity, endurance

TERRAPIN groundedness, wisdom, endurance

SEAL creativity, love, prosperity

WALRUS
shyness,
strength,
touch

SUE COCCIA © 2005

HUMPBACK WHALES

creativity,
family, singing

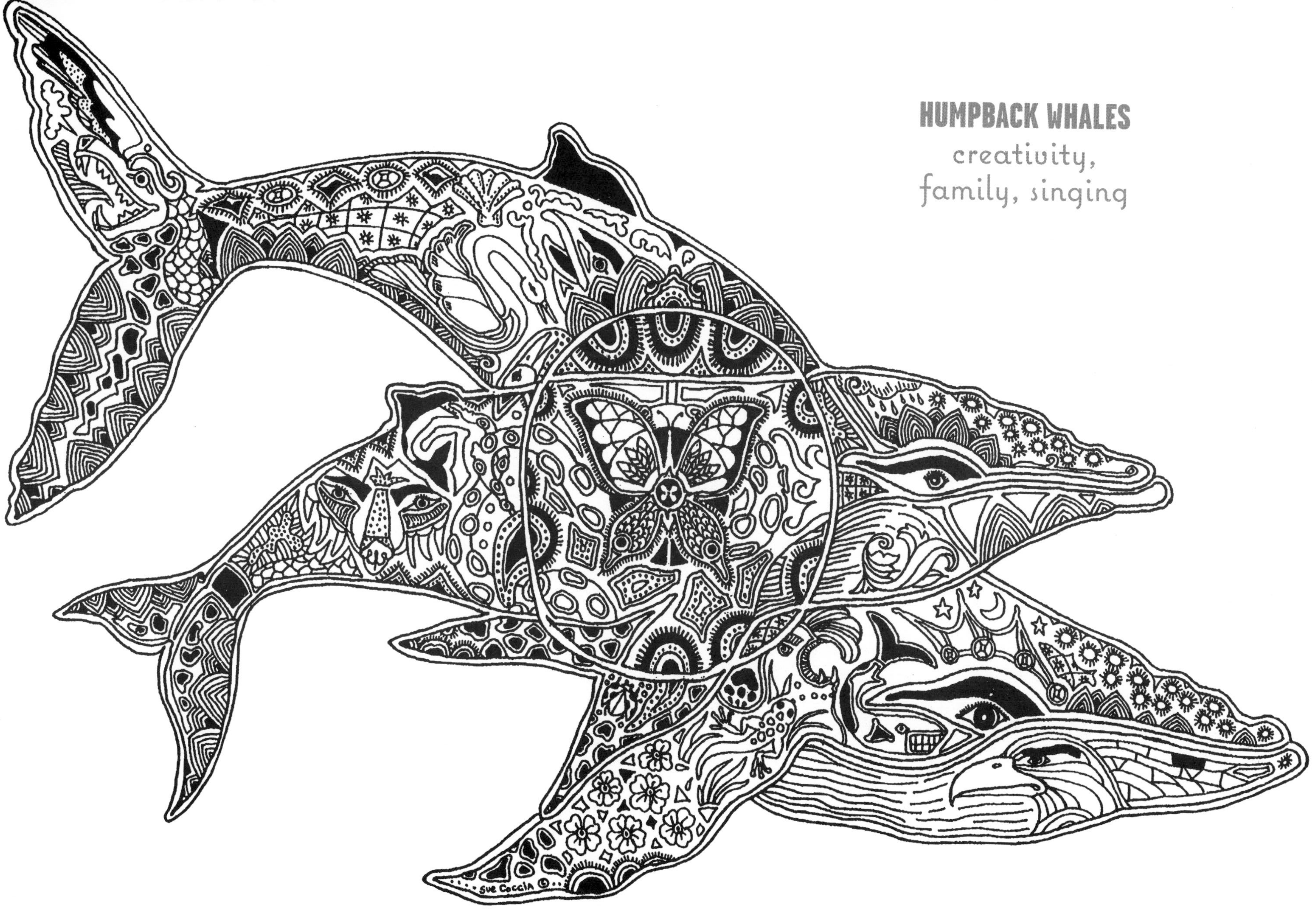

SUE COCCIA ©

POLAR BEAR
wisdom,
power,
the Shaman